BELONGS TO: ______________

LEARNING ARABIC

Journal and Notebook

Made in the USA
Middletown, DE
03 June 2023

32001055R00068